CAMP HOLLIS

CAMP HOLLIS

THE ORIGINS OF OSWEGO COUNTY'S CHILDREN'S CAMP

JIM FARFAGLIA, ALYSA KOLOMS &
JANE ANN SULLIVAN SPELLMAN

THE History PRESS

Published by The History Press
Charleston, SC 29403
www.historypress.net

First published 2008

Manufactured in the United States

ISBN 978.1.59629.582.7

Library of Congress CIP data applied for.

CONTENTS

ACKNOWLEDGEMENTS

The authors would like to thank the following organizations and friends who helped develop this history of Camp Hollis:

Terry Prior, director of the Oswego County Historical Society—Photos, History
The family of Eugene F. and Ruth Reedy Sullivan—Photos, History
The Friends of Camp Hollis—Funding Support
The County of Oswego—Support
New York State Council on Arts/Cultural Resources Council of Syracuse and Onondaga County—Funding Support
The *Palladium-Times*—Newspaper Articles
the river's end bookstore—Book Research
Patricia (McConnell) Pritchard—Photos, History
Dr. David O'Brien—History
Jim Arnold—Photo and Image Preparation
Joanne Familo—Editing
Sandy Davis—Project Advocate

INTRODUCTION

I was honored to be asked by current Camp Hollis director Jim Farfaglia to write an introduction to this new history of Camp Hollis. As the oldest living member of the Eugene Francis and Ruth Reedy Sullivan family, I should be the best person to remember the early years, although my younger brother Mike and his wife Barbara met at Camp Hollis and were on the staff for six years. My older brother Pat (Eugene F. Jr.) served as a counselor, spent two years as director of Camp, and after military service worked with the Camp committee when Daddy was not available. I was a staff member for a short timc and was part of the opening and closing maintenance staff (I just found out I was on a donor list for five dollars—the salary I was never paid). As the historian in the family, I have delved back into the records to remind myself of when the Camp began, to recreate the facts of sixty-two years ago.

When my dad, Eugene F. Sullivan, was elected Oswego County Judge and Children's Court Judge in 1944, he realized that the children who appeared before him were not bad children, but children who had not been given an even chance. Many had responsibilities beyond their years. At that time, there were two orphanages in Oswego, and these children also needed a place to feel special. An outdoor setting where each child could grow and develop in a happy, healthy way would be ideal.

A building on the shores of Lake Ontario—built in 1928 by the Oswego County Health Association (OCHA), a group fighting the dreaded disease of tuberculosis—was not being used. Daddy was a member of the OCHA Board and asked permission to make the building available for a camping program. He realized how much Girl Scout Camp benefited my sister Sheila and me. Daddy knew firsthand the wonderful summers our family had at

Lake Ontario, since his mother-in-law, Anastacia Fogarty Reedy, gave the family a Christmas gift by renting a place on the lake for the summer. The place had a hand pump for water and an outhouse. The lake kept us clean since we spent most of our time in it. We had the joy of outdoor living, where the four Sullivan kids plus friends thrived. Daddy believed the abandoned building that sat on Lewis Bluff represented a chance for other children to have fun.

Establishing a new program for children was a challenge. Vena Stevens, executive director of the Oswego County Girl Scout Council, lent books and advice for running a camp. The OCHA Board and members lent their expertise as well as hours and funds. The immediate job was to get the building, unused for five years, repaired and cleaned. Since the grounds were overgrown, helpful neighbors lent equipment, time and energy to get them in shape.

In 1945, the Oswego County Judge and Children's Court Judge were two part-time positions—two days a week for county court cases and Saturdays for children's court. Daddy's law office in Fulton and our dining room table became spots to sort out application cards, check on medical records, assign bus pickup and notify campers when and where they should wait for buses. While the children's court staff was able to help at times, it was Dad's law office secretary, Anna Mae Scott, who sent mailings, sorted cards and typed lists of campers enrolled. Many of the hours spent were on her own time. Setting up bus routes to pick up campers from all over the county was another time-consuming job.

Then some serious fundraising started. When organizations and individuals learned what the camp was for, the money was donated, but it took time to attend meetings asking for help. The New York State Division for Youth accepted an application for funds and took a chance on this new venture.

With the help of many volunteers, the building was cleaned and equipped. Companies that provided services, such as buses, groceries and milk, were asked to extend credit until the funds arrived. Once the Camp was underway, there were weekly luncheons for the Oswego County Board of Supervisors, civic organizations and individuals who were able to see how much their donations helped. Visitors ate the same meals as the campers and often a performance was given for the groups there. Seeing happy young people enjoying themselves was a satisfying reward for their generosity.

Once the Camp was open, my brother Mike, then age nine, recalls driving out three or four nights a week with his dad to see how things were going. Mike also remembers a Sunday ritual: every other week, they got up early to be at Camp Hollis to take the Catholic campers to church. The Oswego

Knights of Columbus volunteers also were there to get the children to the small chapel nearby. Services for Protestant campers were held in the dining room. Mike reminds me that money ran out the last two weeks of the season and Daddy covered the paychecks for everyone. By 1948, the county support began to stabilize the financial picture. It was still necessary to get support from organizations and individuals, but the allocations from Oswego County and the New York State Division for Youth were an enormous help.

How very proud Daddy would be to see the incredible development of Camp Hollis, now able to serve thousands of children (and adults) without losing the basic belief that a child does develop in a healthy outdoor experience. He loved children and had respect for them, but he also expected them to be responsible and caring individuals. It was worth all the effort to see each child grow in this healthy environment, learning to be on their own, making new friends and believing they were the special people they were. Camp Hollis is a success.

Jane Ann Sullivan Spellman
August 2008

VISIONARY

A Judge's Dream

Camp Hollis, as it is known today, began in 1946 as a recreational haven for many of the region's children. The camp, located on the shores of Lake Ontario in the town of Oswego, derived its name from Dr. LeRoy Hollis of Lacona, New York. Hollis used the site as a health camp from 1928 to 1941. It focused on restoring health to children who were at risk of contracting tuberculosis, then a dreaded disease with no known cure. As Oswego's "Health Camp," it operated under the direction of the Oswego County Health Association, of which Hollis was a guiding force. In 1941, with the cures for tuberculosis becoming more sophisticated and the entire country's efforts turning toward the World War II effort, the camp closed.

Oswego County Judge Eugene F. Sullivan began the action to reopen the camp in the mid-1940s. On January 1, 1945, Sullivan began seven years as Oswego County Court and Children's Court Judge, two part-time positions. Judge Sullivan loved children, and his Saturday morning children's court sessions brought before him many youngsters who were there due to difficult situations at home. Many of these children had responsibilities too great for their years. He took a special interest in the children at the two orphanages—the Oswego Children's Home and the St. Francis Home. Sullivan believed that all children should have a chance to grow and get along with others in a happy setting. Well acquainted with the "magic" of camping along the shores of Lake Ontario, Judge Sullivan began to research the feasibility of creating a program for children who hadn't yet had such an experience.

The judge had been a member of the OCHA Board of Directors, and after many conferences and calls with board members, the decision was made to use the building at Lewis Bluff for a children's camp. A special Camp committee of the OCHA met on June 11, 1946, deciding on two three-week sessions—the first for six- to ten-year-olds, the second for eleven- to thirteen-year-olds. In total, $3,000 was appropriated by the OCHA. Then began the drive to raise the additional funds needed along with the hard work of getting the building in order after several years of neglect.

Once a thriving port city in the late nineteenth and early twentieth centuries, the city of Oswego and the surrounding county had seen some decline by the 1940s. The Great Depression and the war effort stretched resources for so many in the community. Opportunities for recreation and organized youth activities were rare. The county's two orphanages were operating at capacity, and many other children throughout the region were members of struggling families, burdened with responsibilities much greater than could be expected and little time for leisure activities.

Central to Sullivan's vision was his belief that the camp experience should be provided at no charge to the campers' families. This philosophy, adopted and continued throughout the camp's first fifty-eight years, provided an opportunity for all children to be welcome to attend camp. Rather than focusing on the tremendous financial resources needed, Sullivan held fast to the vision of a camp where all were welcome. The monumental task of raising sufficient funds to realize this dream would take time, but complete funding would eventually come.

Shortly before Sullivan began to search for funding, Governor Thomas E. Dewey had appointed an interdepartmental committee to study the problem of juvenile delinquency. This committee's recommendation created the New York State Youth Commission (NYSYC) with a chairman appointed by the governor and the heads of the Departments of Correction, Education, Health, Mental Hygiene and Social Welfare, the Industrial Commissioner and the Chair of the Board of Trade to serve, commencing in 1945. Judge Sullivan was aware of this new group since his wife Ruth was legal counsel at the time to State Senator Isaac B. Mitchell and in Albany during the legislative session. Inquiry was made and the idea that the camp could be used in the prevention of juvenile delinquency was proposed.

A July 13, 1946 news clip from the *Palladium-Times* reported that Robert Kates of the New York State Youth Commission had advised that the

> *Commission had approved the Oswego County Health Camp for participation in state aid under the Youth program. Mr. Kates informed Judge Sullivan that the Oswego County project is the first of this type to be given approval of the Commission. He stated the Commission would regard the local project as an experiment, and if it worked out satisfactorily that another year approval would be given by the Commission.*

This approval for New York State aid would continue through present day.

On July 13, 1946, Dr. LeRoy Hollis died, and at the August 1 meeting of the OCHA, Judge Sullivan recommended the camp be named "Camp Hollis" in memory of this special person who had served as an officer and director of the OCHA for more than twenty-five years and led the organization in building the Camp. The Health Camp was called Camp Hollis in an August 12, 1946 newspaper story and was used in the sign constructed the next year.

Recreation was the essence of what Sullivan wanted for Camp Hollis's campers. What children were able to garner from his vision developed far beyond simple play. Stories told decades after attending the camp demonstrate the deep impact that Sullivan's camp had on these youngsters. Over the years, for thousands of children, Camp Hollis has been their summer vacation, their special memory to share with teachers and fellow students on the first day of school. Among these thousands, Camp Hollis has shown many children a better way of life. It may be that Sullivan's greatest contribution to the legacy that would become Camp Hollis was his determination to provide a recreational outlet that served those who would not have had such an experience otherwise. Judge Eugene F. Sullivan's vision for a camp where children were believed in and could believe in themselves came true in countless ways that he could have never imagined.

The Camp Hollis story begins with Dr. LeRoy Hollis. Hollis, in conjunction with the Oswego County Health Association, first opened the camp's facilities in 1928 as a summer haven for children stricken with or at risk of contracting tuberculosis.

Above: The onset of World War II, coupled with the more advanced treatments for the disease, caused the camp to close in 1941. The campgrounds sat dormant and unattended as the health camp's operations were suspended. Most thought the camp would fade into obscurity.

Left: Judge Eugene F. Sullivan of the Oswego County Children's Court thought of a constructive use of the health camp grounds. Continuously exposed to the county's youth in his court system, Sullivan had big plans to rejuvenate Dr. Hollis's initial mission.

Above: A rare picture of Judge Sullivan at the camp's popular dance, the Hollis Hop. Judge Sullivan became the camp's unofficial photographer and, more often than not, was seen behind a camera rather than in the action.

Right: Judge Sullivan was a prominent figure in the Oswego County political arena. Always an advocate for children's welfare, it is no surprise that Sullivan and his wife Ruth became proactively involved with the use of the abandoned health camp. His county connections and tireless persistence were rewarded through the reopening of the health camp.

Left: Since the camp had been left idle for some time, there was much work to be done. The camp, on a bluff overlooking Lake Ontario and surrounded by woods, was in much need of repair.

Below: Sullivan sought to create a fully equipped and fully functioning summer camp for the children of Oswego County. The judge would work in conjunction with school nurses, orphanages and police departments in order to find children eligible to attend.

In the camp's first year, financial assistance was secured from the Oswego County Health Association. The New York State Youth Commission awarded the camp a "first of its kind" grant for a preventive youth program. Through these and other ways, Sullivan secured the trust and confidence of the county.

Strong community support from county officials, organizations and individuals helped Camp Hollis become ready, fresh and welcoming for its first campers.

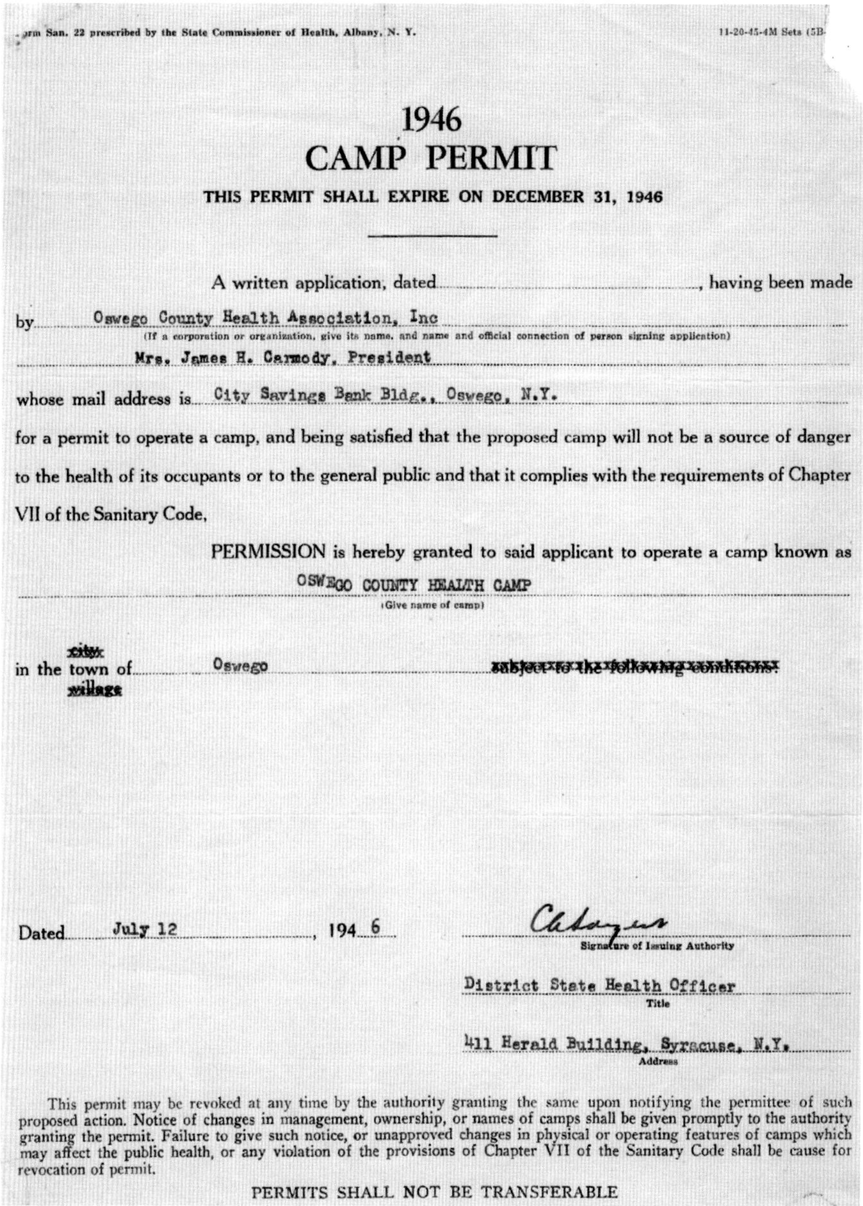

Form San. 22 prescribed by the State Commissioner of Health, Albany, N. Y. 11-20-45-4M Sets (5B-

1946
CAMP PERMIT

THIS PERMIT SHALL EXPIRE ON DECEMBER 31, 1946

A written application, dated ...., having been made

by Oswego County Health Association, Inc
(If a corporation or organization, give its name, and name and official connection of person signing application)
Mrs. James H. Carmody, President

whose mail address is City Savings Bank Bldg., Oswego, N.Y.

for a permit to operate a camp, and being satisfied that the proposed camp will not be a source of danger to the health of its occupants or to the general public and that it complies with the requirements of Chapter VII of the Sanitary Code,

PERMISSION is hereby granted to said applicant to operate a camp known as

OSWEGO COUNTY HEALTH CAMP
(Give name of camp)

in the ~~city~~ town ~~village~~ of Oswego ~~subject to the following conditions:~~

Dated July 12, 1946

C. A. Sayers
Signature of Issuing Authority

District State Health Officer
Title

411 Herald Building, Syracuse, N.Y.
Address

This permit may be revoked at any time by the authority granting the same upon notifying the permittee of such proposed action. Notice of changes in management, ownership, or names of camps shall be given promptly to the authority granting the permit. Failure to give such notice, or unapproved changes in physical or operating features of camps which may affect the public health, or any violation of the provisions of Chapter VII of the Sanitary Code shall be cause for revocation of permit.

PERMITS SHALL NOT BE TRANSFERABLE

With resources in place, campers came for two three-week camp sessions. The health permit shown here was issued to the Oswego County Health Association, granting its support of the operation.

Form San. 62 prescribed by State Commissioner of Health, Albany, N. Y. 2-2-50-5M sets (9B-1146)

APPLICATION FOR RENEWAL OF PERMIT TO OPERATE A CAMP

TO THE DISTRICT STATE HEALTH OFFICER, OR
THE COUNTY COMMISSIONER OF HEALTH, OR
THE CITY COMMISSIONER OF HEALTH

June 21, 19 52
(Date of application)

Sir:

Under the provisions of Chapter VII of the Sanitary Code, application is hereby made for the renewal of the permit to operate a camp, during the year 1952, concerning which the following information is submitted;

Camp location: County Oswego Town ~~Village~~ ~~City~~ Oswego (cross out words not applying)

Camp name Camp Hollis Camp phone 3004-J4 (exchange) (number)

Post office address of camp R. D. # 3, Oswego, New York

Name and mail address of persons or organization operating camp Camp Hollis Committee, County Building, Oswego, New York

Name and address of all organizations occupying camp Camp Hollis Committee, Oswego, N. Y.

Name of organization covered by this application Camp Hollis Committee

Name of individual responsible for camp sanitation Charles Kaine, Director of Camp

Name of milk dealer supplying milk to camp Oswego Netherland Co., Inc., Oswego, N.Y.

Date camp opens June 23, 1952 Date camp closes August 30, 1952

Type of camp Vacation (tourist, labor, vacation, other) for children (adults, children or both)

Total number of persons who used this camp last year about 2200

Camp can accommodate at any one time sixty guests and fifteen employees

Does camp accommodate children under 16 years of age? yes

If so, give name of person responsible for care Charles Kaine, Director of Camp.

State what **changes, if any,** have been made, since the last permit was issued, in the following items. (Write "NONE" for each item not changed)

(a) Camp name None (state former name)

(b) Operator None (state name former operator)

RETAIN THIS COPY FOR YOUR FILE

(OVER)

The success of Camp Hollis became apparent after its first summer. With each successful summer season, community support grew. Working closely with regulatory agencies was an assurance that the camp was operating per state and local health codes.

Judge Sullivan's family shared his passion for the development of the youth camp. Front row: Pat Sullivan, Ruth Reedy Sullivan and Judge Eugene Sullivan. *Back row*: Jane Ann Sullivan, Mike Sullivan and Sheila Sullivan.

So dedicated was Judge Sullivan to the success of Camp Hollis that he would often personally drive the camp vehicle all over the county to pick up campers who were not serviced by the bus.

COOPERATIVE EXTENSION WORK
IN
AGRICULTURE AND HOME ECONOMICS
STATE OF NEW YORK

NEW YORK STATE COLLEGE OF AGRICULTURE
N. Y. STATE COLLEGE OF HOME ECONOMICS
U. S. DEPARTMENT OF AGRICULTURE
OSWEGO CO. FARM AND HOME BUREAU
AND 4-H CLUB ASSOCIATION
COOPERATING

EXTENSION WORK
COUNTY 4-H CLUB AGENT WORK
COURT HOUSE, PULASKI, N. Y.
PHONE 287

March 26, 1952

Judge Eugene Sullivan
Oswego, N. Y.

Dear Judge Sullivan:

The Oswego County 4-H Club Executive Committee approved week-end camping for 4-H members in 1952. It was also suggested that the camp be used two week-ends if possible.

The week-ends of July 6 and 19th would fit into our calendar of summer work very well. We are counting on an arrangement similar to last year if that was satisfactory to you.

Thanks a lot for the opportunity of camping.

Sincerely yours,

William H Cheney

William H. Cheney
County 4-H Club Agent

WHC:B

Eager to see the camp used as much as possible, Sullivan and the camp staff worked to bring organized youth groups to the facility. An agreement between the Camp and 4-H of Oswego County illustrates the long association between the two youth-serving organizations.

The original stationary boasts the Camp Hollis treasure, Lake Ontario. The lake was where many campers had their first swim and learned water skills and safety lessons.

The entire grounds, pictured here, were certainly a sight to see. Pictures like these were used as postcards for campers to write to their families. It helped people throughout Oswego County realize that the campgrounds were clean and safe for their children to attend.

The building itself consisted of a dining area that separated the girls' and boys' wings, with appropriate staff quarters at the end of each wing. Pictured here is the girls' wing with adjoining arts and crafts porch.

The boys' dorm, located on the opposite side of the main building, was a stone's throw away from Lake Ontario. One male camper remembered sleeping in the dorm and feeling the mist from the lake at night.

By the mid-1950s, the site of the Camp Hollis building had to be drastically changed because of its location. Due to bluff erosion, the camp building itself became severely threatened.

The building was dangerously close to the edge of the bluff and shoreline. Severe storms and heavy waves often flooded the roadway into camp. Therefore, it was required that the building be moved in order to save it from falling over the cliff.

In the fall of 1955, work began to move the building farther inland. The building was divided into sections and moved. Transporting large sections of the thirty-year-old wooden structure was delicate work. Happily, after the move, Camp Hollis was still able to operate effectively.

After camp, many parents wrote Judge Sullivan to thank him for their children's summer of fun. Along with Sullivan, the staff received many letters from parents and children thanking them for providing such great memories.

Camp Hollis provided campers with an opportunity to meet many other children and enjoy their company in the outdoors.

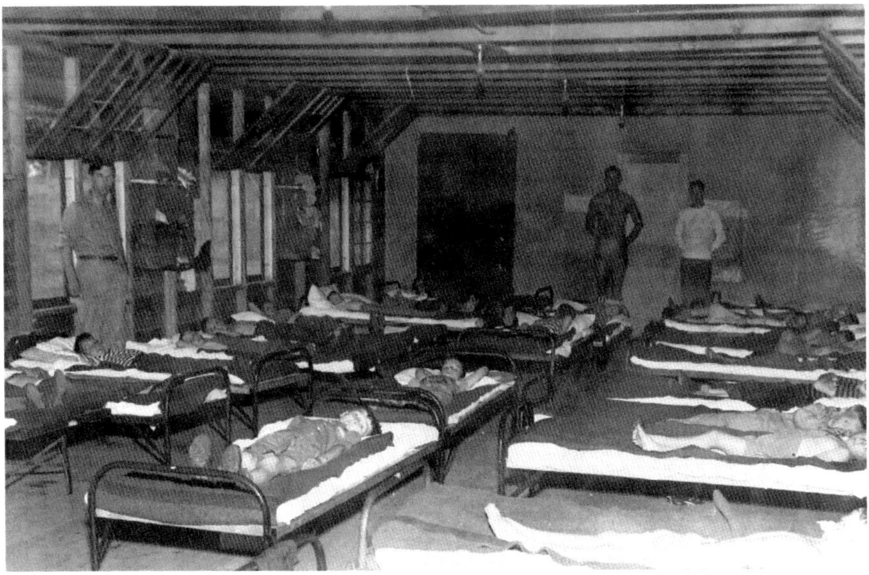

It was also an opportunity for staff and campers to interact with one another. Being away from home and functioning independently was another important growing experience.

Oswego County had few recreational outlets for its young people. Camp Hollis provided a unique experience, aptly stated by Keith Greeney, who attended Camp Hollis in 1953 and 1954: "For what Oswego County wasn't, Camp Hollis was."

The magic of Lake Ontario added to the sense of worth that all felt—camper, staff, volunteer and county and state official. Judge Sullivan's vision established a legacy that continues to this day.

ANGELS

The Camp's Community of Support

While the vision of one man started the drive to open Camp Hollis, it took a community of support to realize the dream. His duties as Children's Court Judge helped Sullivan develop strong work ties with local schools, social service agencies, police departments and churches. His wife Ruth's employment as legal counsel to a New York State senator brought an awareness of innovative initiatives, from which new programs such as Camp Hollis could benefit. Once news of the Camp's mission and altruistic philosophy were announced, volunteer support from the community came forward.

It helped tremendously to have the treasurer and business manager of the *Palladium Times*, E.M. Waterbury, as the camp's publicity chairman. Waterbury made sure that the new camp developing on the shores of Lake Ontario would get ample coverage. Weekly articles offered the community the opportunity to learn firsthand what the pioneer campers were experiencing. Daily schedules were printed—special events were represented with both photos and articles. Funding awarded to the camp was heralded in the news. Stories like the following from 1947 raised concern for the camp and initiated a call for volunteer assistance:

> *Originally, the camp site consisted of about five acres, but it is estimated that about an acre along the lake front has been lost since the camp was established through erosion. The high cliffs in front of the camp has suffered greatly from the effects of the elements and extreme high levels of Lake Ontario that have prevailed for the last two years.*

On the campgrounds sat the building constructed in 1928 by the OCHA. Along with the dining area, the building housed dormitories for boys and girls. Each dormitory contained lavatories and showers. The camp was considered modern as it had a compression tank, heater and a power pump for water. There was a cold storage area in the kitchen that would accommodate a full carcass and all the vegetables required for use at the camp. The kitchen boasted two electric stoves, and drinking water was pumped from the well.

Recruiting campers was another huge job. The OCHA, school nurses, county probation workers, Fulton and Oswego city police officers and social services personnel all offered names of Oswego County residents between the ages of six and thirteen who did not attend another camp. Potential staff members were referred to the camp by various organizations including local city recreation departments. Professors at the nearby Oswego Normal School College promoted the value of working closely with children for its future educators.

Support for the fledging camp was offered in unique ways. The City of Oswego, celebrating its centennial in 1948, asked the camp to participate in its annual Labor Day parade. The float, constructed by staff and volunteers, bore a huge sign stating, "Camp Hollis, For Oswego County Kids." Campers and staff marched together in colorful T-shirts. Through community events such as this, awareness of Camp Hollis grew.

With Sullivan's persistence, the camp became a respected and vital contribution in the region. Knowing of the struggles to raise funds necessary to continue the program, Sullivan continually worked with the Oswego County Board of Supervisors (OCBoS). The OCBoS were the elected supervisors from each town, meeting regularly to conduct county-wide legislation. (The county legislature replaced this body in 1972 with legislators representing districts that crossed township lines.) Sullivan invited the board to the camp often, letting them see firsthand the benefits of their support and the important development that these young children were experiencing. Sullivan prompted OCBoS to consider taking over the supervision of the camp from the Oswego County Health Association, whose responsibilities to the community were changing with the newly organized Oswego County Health Department.

In just a few short years Sullivan had gathered a broad range of community support. A formal resolution of the OCBoS, written at the end of the 1948 season, illustrates the help the new camp was experiencing. The governmental and community agencies, fraternal organizations and individuals who contributed to the success of Camp Hollis included the following:

New York State Youth Commission—$8,546.20
Oswego County Board of Supervisors—$5,000.00
Fulton Community Fund—$1,500.00
Oswego Community Chest—$923.00
Oswego County Health Association—$750.00
Lake City Police Club—$275.00
Fulton Police Benevolent Club—$200.00
Women's Auxiliary, Fulton Chamber of Commerce—$105.00
Fulton Lodge of Elks—$100.00
Auxiliary of the County Medical Association—$50.00 (to purchase small washing machine)
Oswego County Justice's Association—$76.00 (fund for dishes)
Oswego Masonic Club—$75.00
Centennial Committee (Board of Supervisors Fund)—$74.37
Supervisors, Highway Commissioners and Employee's Picnic—$55.00 (toward dishes)
Neil O'Brien Lumber Co.—$50.00
Oswego County Sheriff's Department—$50.00 (toward dishes)
Fulton Ministerial Association—$25.00
Mr. Charles Goldstein, Oswego—$18.00
Mrs. Charles Swain, Fulton—$5.00
Mr. Richard Van Valkenberg—$2.00
Isabell Bower—$0.60

OCBoS decided that a special committee should be named to help with the budgeting of funds available for the operation and maintenance of Camp Hollis. This committee was to consist of the chairman of the Directors of the OCHA and a member of the OCBoS. They were to set salaries and establish policy on distribution of funds for the maintenance and operation of the camp with regard to purchases, repairs, improvements and the like. The wide array of donors illustrates the good will that Camp Hollis was given from its inception and that the community immediately recognized the value of the camp program.

Finally, in 1954, Reverend John Scarlet, president of the OCHA, requested that Oswego County assume responsibility for Camp Hollis. A resolution was passed to create a Recreation Commission and Camp Hollis officially became a part of the Oswego County's governmental structure, where it remains today.

Though secure under the direction of Oswego County, severe storms off of Lake Ontario and the ongoing erosion of the bluff that the camp sat on caused a new challenge for Camp Hollis. The proximity of the building to the bluff caused much concern for the camp's administration. In 1955, the need to relocate the building away from the edge of the eroded bluff was finally addressed by moving the camp back with the support of the U.S. Naval "Seabees" from Liverpool. This was accomplished by cutting the building into three sections and moving it to the new foundation. Campers returning in 1956 were surprised and delighted to see the camp in a new spot.

Judge Sullivan, far right, spent countless hours talking with area leaders to develop community support for the new camp program. The campgrounds were always open for visits from local officials so that they could see firsthand the accomplishments of the camp.

Regularly scheduled luncheons and receptions were provided at the camp by the kitchen staff. State and local representatives were invited to make sure those supporting the camp could realize its benefits.

Help was needed in all areas. The kitchen staff had the responsibility of preparing, serving and cleaning up after three meals and a snack per day. Volunteers were always welcome to lend a hand.

Once the meal was prepared, serving it in a timely fashion was a challenge. Both volunteers and staff served the family-style tables so that children got as much food as they desired. Second and third glasses of milk were always available. Staff and volunteers spent most of the mealtime on their feet and serving.

Volunteers came to the camp through many avenues. Charles Parry, pictured here, was the boyfriend to first-year counselor Norma Clark. He learned of the need for help to supervise and entertain the children through her and was welcomed to the staff as a much-needed extra hand.

Above: The "camp on the bluff" garnered support from the surrounding farmers who were interested in the success of the camp. Neighbors were aware of the magic of what was happening.

Right: The newly developed play area made for a less-than-ideal ball field. Volunteers helped to clear the field of debris, construct the backstop and put in base lines. Soon the campers felt as if they were playing on a league-ranked field.

Also working on the ball field and other projects were parolees from the county jail. Working their community service hours, the men provided manual labor around the campgrounds.

While the children played, local businesses pitched in to help the camp provide all that was necessary for the program. Vendors were eager to work with staff to supply the camp with necessary foods and supplies. Success of the program was foremost in the camp leaders' minds and many in the community supported this.

Above: A local grocer delivers fresh fruit and vegetables to the camp. Vendors or local farmers often shared surplus produce to assist the kitchen staff in offering nutritious meals.

Right: Early in the camp's existence, the decision was made to provide special Camp Hollis T-shirts for campers and staff. Ideas for the logo were offered from the community. Camp Director H.H. Stevens offered his background in the arts and love of the outdoors. The shirt became a well-known image of the camp and the design was used for over thirty years.

One proud moment involving the Camp Hollis T-shirts was the camp's involvement in the City of Oswego's Labor Day parade. Coinciding with the centennial of the city, the 1948 patriotic parade included an invitation for Camp Hollis to participate.

Once the invitation was accepted, work on the float began. Both staff and volunteers lent artistic talent and labor to creating the float. Shown here are counselor Patricia (McConnell) Pritchard and volunteer Bob Bowers, son of the camp's cook.

The float was an intricate design, as was construction. Those in observance of the parade saw the campground in its glory, sitting prominently on the bluffs of Lake Ontario.

Surely, however, the most impressive sight must have been the hundreds of campers who marched behind the float. Dressed in their Camp Hollis T-shirts and singing the familiar songs they had learned at campfires, these children were among the most endearing to the crowds. Many cheered as the staff and campers passed by. The community fell in love with this special program dedicated to its children.

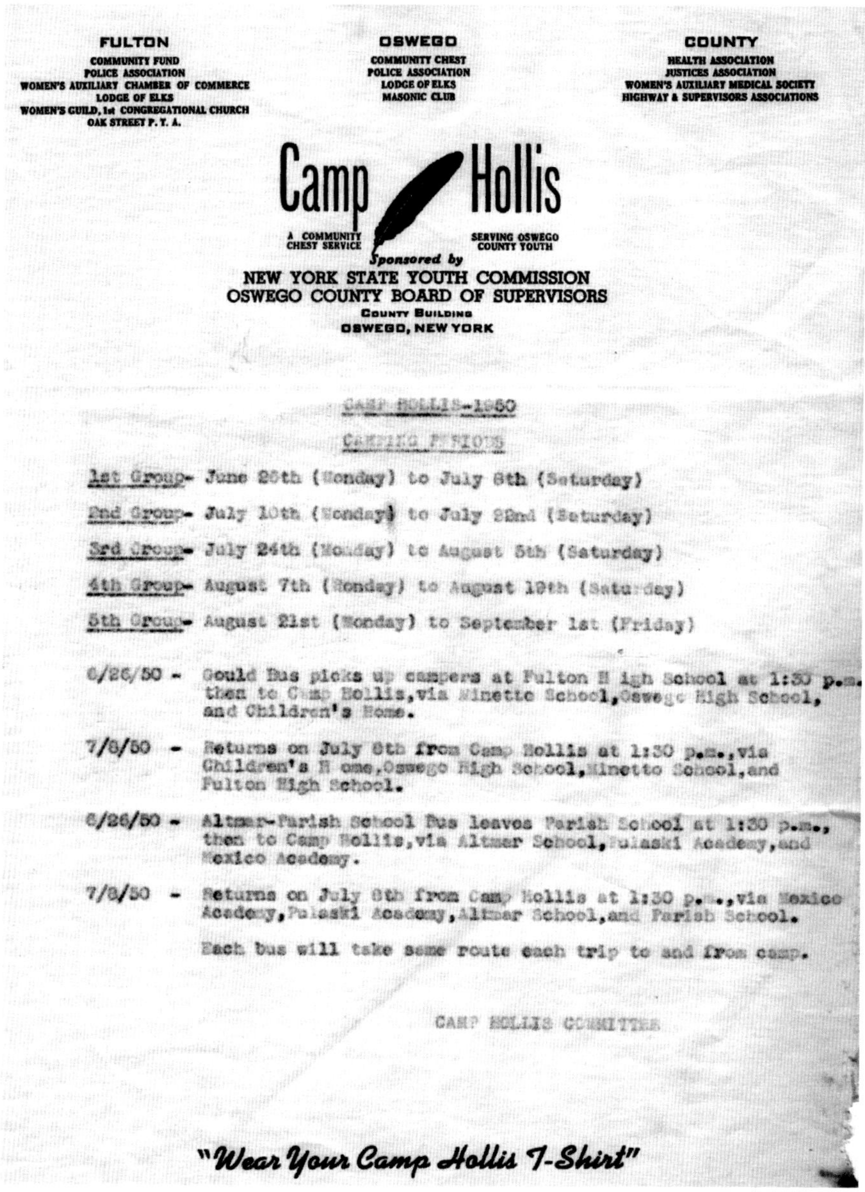

FULTON
COMMUNITY FUND
POLICE ASSOCIATION
WOMEN'S AUXILIARY CHAMBER OF COMMERCE
LODGE OF ELKS
WOMEN'S GUILD, 1st CONGREGATIONAL CHURCH
OAK STREET P. T. A.

OSWEGO
COMMUNITY CHEST
POLICE ASSOCIATION
LODGE OF ELKS
MASONIC CLUB

COUNTY
HEALTH ASSOCIATION
JUSTICES ASSOCIATION
WOMEN'S AUXILIARY MEDICAL SOCIETY
HIGHWAY & SUPERVISORS ASSOCIATIONS

Camp Hollis

A COMMUNITY CHEST SERVICE

SERVING OSWEGO COUNTY YOUTH

Sponsored by
NEW YORK STATE YOUTH COMMISSION
OSWEGO COUNTY BOARD OF SUPERVISORS
COUNTY BUILDING
OSWEGO, NEW YORK

CAMP HOLLIS-1950

CAMPING PERIODS

1st Group- June 26th (Monday) to July 8th (Saturday)

2nd Group- July 10th (Monday) to July 22nd (Saturday)

3rd Group- July 24th (Monday) to August 5th (Saturday)

4th Group- August 7th (Monday) to August 19th (Saturday)

5th Group- August 21st (Monday) to September 1st (Friday)

6/26/50 - Gould Bus picks up campers at Fulton H igh School at 1:30 p.m. then to Camp Hollis, via Minetto School, Oswego High School, and Children's Home.

7/8/50 - Returns on July 8th from Camp Hollis at 1:30 p.m., via Children's H ome, Oswego High School, Minetto School, and Fulton High School.

6/26/50 - Altmar-Parish School Bus leaves Parish School at 1:30 p.m., then to Camp Hollis, via Altmar School, Pulaski Academy, and Mexico Academy.

7/8/50 - Returns on July 8th from Camp Hollis at 1:30 p.m., via Mexico Academy, Pulaski Academy, Altmar School, and Parish School.

Each bus will take seme route each trip to and from camp.

CAMP HOLLIS COMMITTEE

"Wear Your Camp Hollis T-Shirt"

Another community supporter was Frank "Dynamite" Gould, who owned a local bus company. He worked with Judge Sullivan to accommodate the transportation of all the campers with pickup routes placed throughout Oswego County. Shown here is the agreement with Gould's Bus Company and Camp Hollis for a season of service.

Frank L. Gould --- Bus Lines
158 West Second Street
Oswego, New York

Telephone 978

September 1, 1950

Eugene F. Sullivan, Judge Oswego County
Oswego County Building
46 East Bridge Street
Oswego, New York

Dear Judge Sullivan:

Enclosed you will find Oswego County Bill Forms in triplicate which have been signed and notarized, also our original bill No. 060 in the amount of fifteen dollars ($15.00) which covers transportation of children from Camp Hollis to St. Mary's Mission and return Sunday July 16, 1950 and our bill No. 061 covering Seasonal Charter to Camp Hollis in the amount of three hundred dollars ($300.00).

Very truly yours,
FRANK L. GOULD BUS LINES

By Peggy Tynan
Bookkeeper

p
encls. 8

Sullivan worked with local and state officials and community charitable organizations to raise the funds. Bills for the services were often presented with a note to "pay when possible." Because of the generosity of many vendors, the camp was able to concentrate on serving the children first and acquire and allocate funds after.

The bus ride to and from camp was a memorable one for the children. Many had never left home before and few had traveled to Lake Ontario. Shown in this picture are campers returning home after their two-week stay. Donning their brand-new Camp Hollis T-shirts, many eagerly awaited being reunited with their families and friends to share their memories of the camp.

SHEPHERDS

The Staff

The Camp Hollis staff members in the early years of the camp had the responsibility to bring to reality Judge Sullivan's vision. The choice of H.H. Stevens, who served as Camp Hollis director from 1946 to 1950, was a fortunate one. Stevens, principal of the Minetto, New York elementary school, had a special interest in using the outdoors for educational purposes. While the OCHA Camp committee was putting in long hours to get the building in shape, Stevens, who had previous experience in camp programs, began his work as director. He recruited registered nurse Virginia McNamara-Cullinan as camp nurse and Norma Clark, Helen Longhway, Eunice Nichols, Kenneth Nichols, Clarence McKinstry Jr. and Allan Ranous as counselors. Mrs. Hilda Brown, who was the cook at the Fort Ontario Officers Club from 1940 to 1945, took on the all-important position of cook. Irene and Charlotte Courtwright were assistants in the kitchen. William Brown was camp custodian, although counselors and volunteers did much of the maintenance.

By the time Robert Bellinger, director from 1956 to 1959, hired his staff, it included ten counselors (five male and five female), one cook, three kitchen girls, one nurse and one handyman. His wife Barbara also worked at the camp, helping him with director's duties. The staff handled the thirty girls and thirty boys that came to camp every two weeks. Bellinger stated, "We surely didn't do this job for the pay. Counselors made $200 for ten weeks of work. Pay was every two weeks. As a consolation for low pay, the camp arranged for the counselors to have cube steaks and Coke for their evening snacks."

In the early years of Camp, the staff came from the Oswego County region, mainly from the Oswego Normal School, a teachers college that was located a few miles from the campgrounds. Work at a children's camp was fruitful employment for the future educators, and many supplemented their classroom studies with hands-on work as a counselor at Camp Hollis. What a rich experience for future teachers!

Working to provide entertaining recreational activities using limited resources on largely undeveloped grounds was a monumental task. Counselors learned to lead the camp by referring to their own experiences, memories of games and activities they enjoyed as children and from ideas acquired in their teaching classes. While some counselors received special training to become certified swim instructors, archery range leaders and boating instructors, many programs that became camper favorites were created on the spot. Using the resources available, such as the lake, the beach, the woods (with its primitive trail system) and basic recreation equipment, the responsibility of creating fun for the children became the staff's impassioned task.

Given the limited number of staff and the grand scale of work needed for the program to succeed, the staff often had multiple hats to wear. Counselors were not only responsible for the caretaking of the children, but also many miscellaneous tasks around the camp. Maintenance of both the grounds and weather-worn building; security of the camp both day and night; helping to prepare, serve and clean up after meals—all became part of their busy jobs.

Summers as a counselor created a lifetime of memories as Joanie Koster Mayhew, on staff from 1952 to 1956, relates her string of recollections:

> *Pat Sullivan listening to Dave Brubeck records; Mrs. DeBello making special meals for the visitors Judge Sullivan would bring (he was trying to get donations to keep Camp open); singing songs around the campfire; children coming to the Camp who had never had all the milk that they wanted to drink before; some kids were afraid to eat Jell-O because it moved; collecting used kid's clothes from everyone I knew for the kids at Camp; working two weeks, leaving camp on Saturday afternoon to go home, do laundry, regroup and come back again Sunday night or Monday morning; the year it rained all the time, we had to take the kids on "rainy day hikes" everyday to keep them busy; standing in the water making a human chain so the children could go swimming, it was rough and freezing; playing bingo; putting on shows; writing a camp song; the children we had with special needs.*

The social life was an added benefit to the employment package. There was a potential for some interesting times for a staff of male and female young adults after all the kids were in bed by 10:00 p.m. Future husbands and wives met on the shores of Lake Ontario while working together as counselors at Camp Hollis. Friendships that lasted a lifetime were forged as the staff worked to create happy memories for children.

Becoming surrogate parents for the children while they were at the camp was a great challenge for the counselors. Many of the staff were just entering young adulthood, and had only recently felt the responsibility of their lives shift from their parents to themselves. To suddenly be given the care of young children was a huge undertaking. The staff created daily schedules and routines for the day to help with the task of properly supervising the youngsters. Incentives to encourage participation in daily camp cleanup and maintenance were initiated. In the course of a summer, counselors learned the elements of effective child care. By the end of the summer, many young adults became proficient child care providers.

No matter how staff members found their way to Camp Hollis, they came with one thing in common—a love and concern for children. No one worked at Camp Hollis to make a lot of money. It also allowed for only rare occasions of free time. Counselors gave up their own summers of relaxation and youthful fun to become caretakers for children who were in need of attention and enjoyment. Robert Friel, a counselor in 1958, recalls, "I realize how much I enjoyed working and helping those who were not as fortunate as many in Oswego County. It was the beginning of my social conscience being awakened. It was also challenging working with 12 and 13 year olds when I was a mere unchallenged 17 year old!"

The impact of the staff on the campers was often life changing. Some campers' homes were often so busy with the tasks at hand that there was no time for a child's recreational needs. Children from two orphanages and within the social service system often lacked consistent, positive role models. Camp Hollis's counselors were able to give children what so many dearly lacked. From the perspective of a young and impressionable camper, staff were often emulated and seen as idols. Years after leaving Hollis, former campers still recall the names and unique personalities of their favorite counselors.

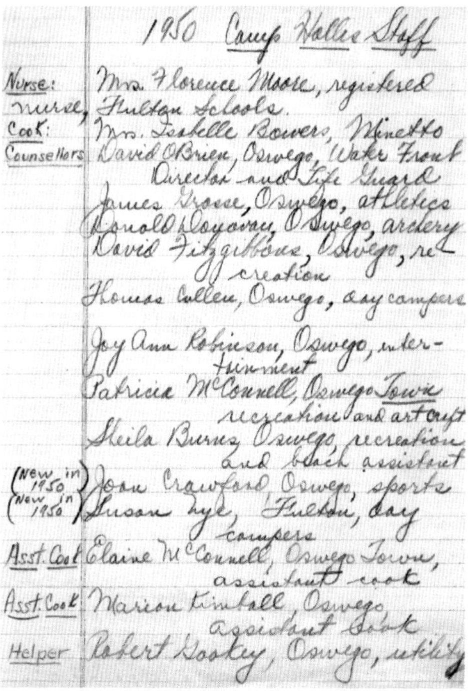

1950 Camp Hollis Staff

Nurse: Mrs. Florence Moore, registered nurse, Fulton Schools.

Cook: Mrs. Isabelle Bowers, Minetto

Counsellors: David O'Brien, Oswego, Water Front Director and Life Guard

James Grosse, Oswego, athletics

Donald Doyavan, Oswego, archery

David Fitzgibbons, Oswego, recreation

Thomas Cullen, Oswego, day campers

Joy Ann Robinson, Oswego, entertainment

Patricia McConnell, Oswego Town recreation and art craft

Sheila Burns, Oswego, recreation and beach assistant

(New in 1950) Joan Crawford, Oswego, sports

(New in 1950) Susan Nye, Fulton, day campers

Asst. Cook: Elaine McConnell, Oswego Town, assistant cook

Asst. Cook: Marion Kimball, Oswego, assistant cook

Helper: Robert Gookey, Oswego, utility

Above: To be a counselor at Camp Hollis certainly took a very special type of individual. Pictured here are the counselors from the first summer of camp.

Left: Developing the staff each year was an important part in the camp's progress. One by one, the staff members were hired and lists were compiled. Oftentimes the judge would write lists of things to remember or do in between court sessions.

As the years progressed, funding increased and the staff size grew to more adequately address the needs of the campers. Pictured here is the entire staff of the summer of 1951. Front row: Mrs. Florence Moore, camp nurse; Vivian Kimball; Marian Russell; Barbara Main; Adeline Mirandes; Joan Sullivan; Patricia McConnell; Elaine Weske; and Mrs. Florence Roff. Back row: Charles Kaine, camp director at the time; David Fitzgibbons; Thomas Drumm; Thomas Tovey; William Kessler; David O'Brien; and Richard Doney.

The camp director had the responsibility for the campers, staff, building and grounds. Pictured here is Bob Bellinger, director from 1956 to 1959.

Pat Sullivan, the judge's oldest son, served as a counselor in 1947; after military service, he was camp director from 1954 to 1955.

Right: Staff at Camp Hollis enjoyed precious few moments to relax and rarely enjoyed a full day off. Here are a few counselors relaxing in the sun during a moment of cherished free time at camp.

Below: The back porch off the kitchen was a favorite spot for counselors to take a break. The reward of the countless staff and volunteers who assisted in the camp's first year was in knowing that they were participating in a project that both enhanced and benefited their community.

The kitchen was the core of the camp. Long hours in the kitchen provided the essential ingredient of the camp's success. Those who cooked the meals recall looking out the kitchen window and watching the children playing and swimming while they wiped away sweat working over a hot stove. It was a reminder that it took many talents to operate a successful camp.

Right down the road from Camp Hollis was the Oswego Teachers College, now the State University of New York at Oswego. Camp Hollis was a wonderful opportunity of experience for the college's students interested in education.

Right: Many of the counselors who came to Camp Hollis in its first years were not acquainted with one another before their work there began. Soon, through the bond that is created when caring for children, lifelong friendships and relationships began.

Below: While many counselors enjoyed leading games and activities, they also were promoting safety precautions. Regular staff meetings were held in the dining hall as ongoing training.

The counselors, as child care providers, strove to give the children their utmost care and caution. While some of this came from formal training, they also began to develop good judgment and common sense.

Camp staff knew little of each child's background. All were treated equally.

Counselors were well aware of the Camp Hollis mission. Many of the counselors in the earlier years understood the importance of Camp Hollis and its place within the community. Everything from organizing morning cleanup in the dorms to planning creative craft projects made a difference in the children's lives.

Above: Patricia (McConnell) Pritchard, a counselor from 1948 to 1952, stated: "Many children did not have a chance to go to camp or have a vacation any other way. That was Judge Sullivan's purpose, a lot of them needed something positive in their life and Camp Hollis was the answer to that problem." Pictured here are Pritchard and counselor Bill Kessler with a group of children.

Right: Counselors often had trouble believing that they were getting paid to have such fun. While responsibilities were great, the opportunities for fun and fellowship were many. Two counselors watch their campers swimming on a summer day.

Left: Staff developed as a strong team by working side by side toward a common goal. Friends and family "back home" noticed a change in these impassioned young adults.

Below: Staff learned as much from the campers as the campers learned from them. Having only their own family situations as reference points, staff members were often surprised to learn about the many different ways others had been raised.

Richard Bateman, who attended Camp Hollis in 1953, remembers: "My recollection of the counselors was that they were people who were caring people."

While counselors certainly imparted valuable lessons to their campers, campers also gave lifelong lessons to their counselors. Many staff chose child-caring professions and referred to Camp Hollis as the reason for their choice.

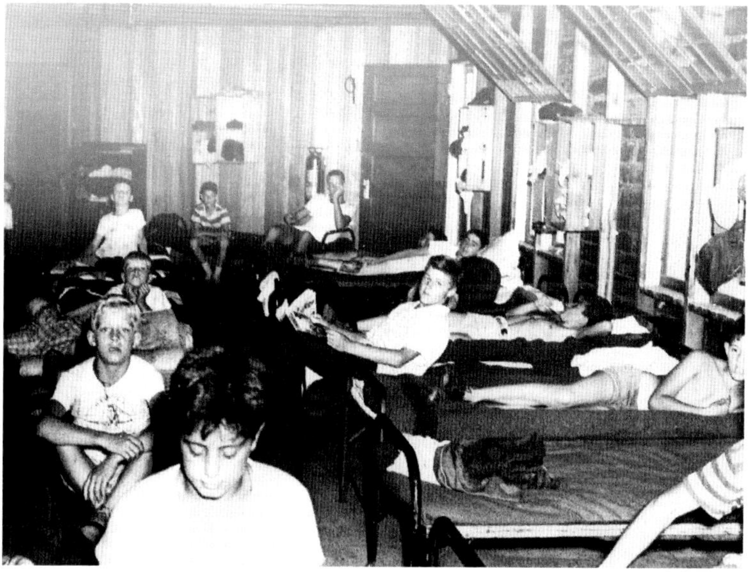

The rest period was an important part of the day's schedule, and was required for both campers and counselors. Since the daily schedule stretched for over fourteen hours, a break from the activities was necessary. Shelter from the sun in the heat of the day was a welcome reprieve for many.

The counselors from the early staff at Camp Hollis spent many hours developing a variety of legends, many of which exist today. Mike Sullivan remembers taking campers for a hike along Snake Swamp Road. Sullivan recalls that he and John Kessler pointed out a newly tarred road with sets of footprints in it. The group was told that they were footprints of "George." Taking this lead, counselors created the "Legend of George Hollis," which has evolved through the years.

A group of male counselors wrote a skit about the George Hollis legend for Camp Hollis's skit night. Pictured here are Tom Cullen, Bill Kessler, Frank Cullen, David O'Brien (with a stocking over his face, playing George Hollis) and Jim Grose.

The activities coupled with the lessons learned during the summers positioned the counselors as role models for many of the campers.

Above: As role models, counselors were constantly observed and imitated. For staff members in their late teens, this was a big responsibility.

Left: The responsibility of being a proper role model was also passed on to the next generation.

Right: Counselors, many years after their employment, are approached by past campers, who expressed deep gratitude for providing such wonderful summers.

Below: Regardless of their expectations of what they would find at Camp Hollis, the staff ended their summers knowing they had participated in something special. Many counselors, like campers, would return to Camp Hollis year after year.

David O'Brien, on staff from 1948 to 1952, and Allan Ranous, 1946–48, were among the dedicated staff members from the camp's first years.

Mike Sullivan, the judge's youngest son, worked four summers at the camp, several of those as waterfront director. He fondly remembers the work at Camp Hollis being about the children: "They were responsive, loving, grateful and excited. Because for almost all it was the first and only time they'd experienced such things."

PIONEERS

Hollis's First Campers

On July 8, 1946, twenty-seven boys and twenty-seven girls from all over Oswego County got off buses to begin a new adventure. These children were pioneers, the first to attend a residential camp for children who otherwise would never enjoy such an experience. The first campers, and the thousands who followed, came from a wide variety of home and community environments. Many campers were from families burdened with poverty and so, at a young age, were given responsibilities much greater than one could expect a child to handle. Others suffered loss and a lack of security at a young age. No matter what conditions a child came from, once these children arrived at Camp Hollis, the hardships were put aside. The Camp Hollis community welcomed and cared for all.

Recruiting campers to attend an unknown program was a huge job. Working with Lucy Vincent, the OCHA nurse, the County Probation Department, Fulton and Oswego Police Departments, the Oswego Children's Home, St. Francis Children's Home (in Oswego) and social services personnel, names were given of eligible children.

Mailings to these children and taking the return reservations were done on Judge Sullivan's dining room table the first few years. Bus pickups were arranged, and letters were sent to campers regarding what to bring and where to be picked up for the bus. Many of the families involved did not have telephones and it required driving to houses in the out-of-the-way places to see if the children would be coming. Of course, there was resistance to something unknown. In that first year, it might require a court order for the parents to "agree" to send their children. This never happened after the first year, when campers went home with happy tales of their adventures.

By 1948, the camp was so full that many children interested in attending were asked to participate in a day program at the campground. Day campers from Hannibal, Mexico and Minetto, as well as Oswego and Fulton recreation groups, used the campsite. The 4-H and police departments also sponsored regular programs.

Staff members worked hard to create an environment where each child mattered. Temporarily away from the hardships of life and a sometimes harsh world, campers were provided activities and programs that demonstrated a welcoming and encouraging existence. For the children who attended, it was simply great opportunity.

The impact of the camp on its campers was immense. Whether children were able to attend for one summer or several, Camp Hollis made a lasting impression. Two or three weeks of unrestricted fun for a child who had never had that opportunity was quite the experience. To be a child accustomed to life devoid of many cultural and recreational opportunities, Camp Hollis was seen as a haven. Many years later, former campers shared their memories of the program, mixing the wonder of a child with the mature perspective of an adult.

Valuable life lessons were a part of the daily activities at Camp Hollis. Working together as a team was not only found in the daily baseball games but also in the dormitories during morning cleanup time. Tolerance for those different from you came to life when a bunkmate shared experiences that were new and exciting. A child without siblings suddenly had twenty or thirty brothers and sisters, and the lessons of sharing and waiting for turns became a necessity. During each fun-filled day, without knowing it, campers became aware of how to be a responsible, respectful and caring individual. What was taught at home and at school was reinforced at Camp Hollis.

For many, being away from home was a first-time experience. Both parent and child felt the pangs of separation and, for some, this memory would have a lasting effect on their perception of the camp. Many children wrote postcards home in the first days of the session begging to be picked up. Counselors worked hard to convince children of the importance of staying and working through those homesick feelings. With time and perspective, many saw the value of experiencing those difficult first few days. Attending residential camp was often a first step of a person developing individual identity. Away from parents, children learned to rely on themselves, and realized that they could make friends and find comfort in new environments.

The importance of being a camper at Camper Hollis and what it meant to a child's development has been discussed for years. Former campers report that they did indeed retain those lessons learned on the baseball field, on the playground, in the water and at the meal table. Many campers, filled with memories from their Camp Hollis experience, became staff members. Some grew up to be teachers, nurses or social workers. Most became loving and attentive parents, aunts, uncles and siblings.

FULTON	OSWEGO	COUNTY
COMMUNITY FUND POLICE ASSOCIATION WOMEN'S AUXILIARY CHAMBER OF COMMERCE LODGE OF ELKS WOMEN'S GUILD, 1st CONGREGATIONAL CHURCH OAK STREET P. T. A.	COMMUNITY CHEST POLICE ASSOCIATION LODGE OF ELKS MASONIC CLUB	HEALTH ASSOCIATION JUSTICES ASSOCIATION WOMEN'S AUXILIARY MEDICAL SOCIETY HIGHWAY & SUPERVISORS ASSOCIATIONS

Camp Hollis

A COMMUNITY CHEST SERVICE

SERVING OSWEGO COUNTY YOUTH

Sponsored by

NEW YORK STATE YOUTH COMMISSION
OSWEGO COUNTY BOARD OF SUPERVISORS
COUNTY BUILDING
OSWEGO, NEW YORK

Hello, Camper:

Summer is near which means Camp Hollis!

Fill out the enclosed card at once, and then have 'Dad' or 'Mom' sign it and return the card filled out. Mail it immediately. If you are unable to attend, please so state on the card and return it anyway. Remember! Do it NOW!

If you can go to Scout Camp or Church Camp or to a camp with your parents, relatives or friends, you should not plan to attend Camp Hollis. Camp Hollis is for boys and girls who will not attend any other camp.

Bring no money with you to camp. There is no need for it and no place to spend it, as you know.

Slacks, shorts, T-shirts, socks, swim trunk or suit, sweater or sweat shirt and sneakers are suggested. Don't get new ones. The old will do. Camp Hollis is for fun.

Don't bring sheets, towels or blankets, or valuable watches, cameras, flashlights and jewelry.

Please do not request same camp period as brother or sister or some 'pal'.

You are assigned to the camp period beginning Monday, June 25th to Saturday, July 7th

If you accept, a card will be sent to you to tell you where and at what hour you are to meet the bus to take to Camp Hollis.

And parents, relatives and friends -- please DON'T VISIT your youngster while he or she is at Camp. Come some other time if you wish.

CAMP HOLLIS COMMITTEE

"Wear Your Camp Hollis T-Shirt"

The camp season began with a mass mailing to those campers who were eligible to attend. As seen in the letter, the Camp Hollis administration placed special emphasis on the insistence that children were not to spend any unnecessary money on materials for camp.

A large part of the camper foundation at Camp Hollis came from the two orphanages in Oswego—the Oswego Children's Home and the St. Francis Home. Many of these children were ultimately placed in orphanages as a result of passing through Judge Sullivan's court. Sullivan was keenly aware of their circumstances.

Principals from regional schools, officials of local churches and administrators of the Oswego County orphanages were among those that comprised the camper selection committee. They surveyed the community to find children who would benefit from the recreation program.

All of the children selected to attend Camp Hollis in the early years could attend for free. Despite providing the camp at no cost, Sullivan still had to help parents understand the benefits of the camp experience for their children.

With the majority of the children coming from homes with limited resources, many of the campers looked at Camp Hollis as simply a great opportunity.

Camp Hollis Committee regrets you cannot be accommodated at the Camp this year. However, you are invited to attend Day Camp on Monday thru Friday, August 23rd, to 27th, if there are other boys desirous of attending. The bus will pick you up at Oak Hill School at about 8:45 AM each day, take you to Camp, lunch free, return home about 4:00 PM, swimming baseball, play. Call Oswego 357, between 9:00 AM - 12:00 Noon and 2:00 PM and 4:00 PM Friday, if you care to attend.

IF YOU ATTEND, THIS CARD WILL BE SHOWN TO BUS DRIVER

FOR ADMITTANCE TO BUS

CAMP HOLLIS COMMITTEE

BE ON TIME, UNLESS YOU HEAR OTHERWISE -

There were only so many beds available and more children wanted to go. Camp Hollis began offering a day camp. Children from several cities, towns and villages attended.

Campers in 1946 were accepted to attend for a three-week period. By 1947, the program had been changed to be three two-week sessions.

Campers ranged from ages six to thirteen years of age. A variety of activities were planned by the staff and a wide range of playground and sports equipment was acquired to challenge and please all age groups attending.

For many campers, their experience at Camp Hollis was the first time away from home. Feelings of homesickness were often a part of a camper's first day or two at the camp. Soon, however, the fun activities and caring staff helped the campers enjoy their time. By the time the session ended, many children shed tears because they did not want to leave.

Some of the campers came to Camp Hollis already knowing others. They were often classmates, neighbors or from the same orphanage. After leaving camp, the youngsters would talk with fondness about their shared experiences at the camp.

A great number of long-lasting friendships were formed. All of the campers shared the common fact that they were experiencing something new, exciting and wonderful.

Structure and organization governed the campers' typical day. Flag raising, various activities, bedtime and meals were all scheduled daily. However, the regimen always allowed for free time!

Campers certainly remembered their time on the waters of Lake Ontario. Along with swimming, campers enjoyed boating, rafting and fishing.

The chance for certified Red Cross swimimg lessons was a unique opportunity for the children. With a Great Lake, several rivers and backyard ponds in the region, learning to swim was vital.

The dormitory aspect of camp was treasured by many of its campers. Campers slept on donated army cots and kept their belongings in orange crates that, as can be seen, were kept mounted on the wall. The dorm-style arrangement allowed up to thirty girls in one wing of the building and thirty boys in the other.

Camp Hollis's first director, H.H. Stevens, gathers with a small group of the camp's first campers. He was principal of the Minetto Elementary School, a local school in the Oswego County region. Stevens, in the 1940s and '50s, gave up his summers to run the camp.

Mealtime was extremely important. Fresh food, professionally prepared, was a treat for all of the children but especially for those without proper nutrition at home. Many of the campers interviewed in later years commented on the joy of being able to eat to their satisfaction.

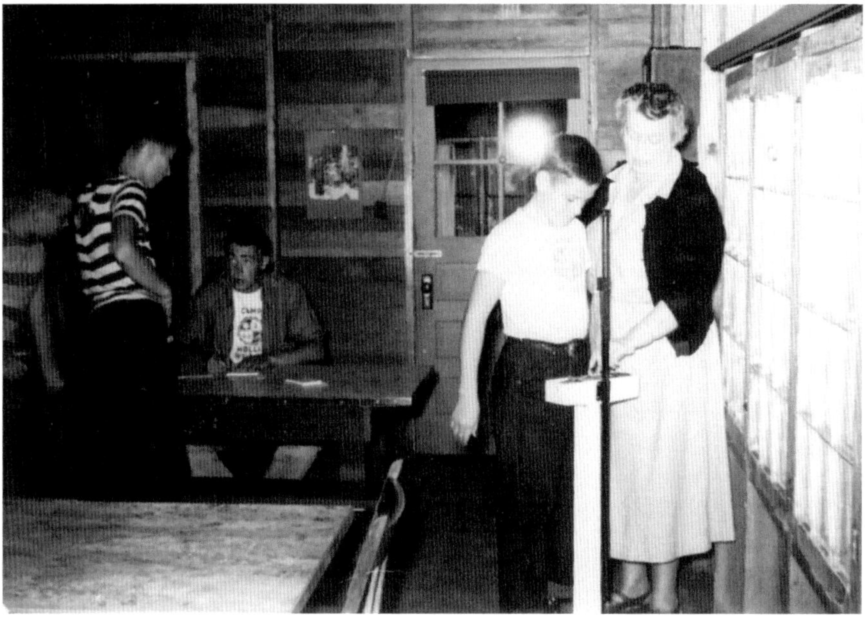

Many of the campers came from homes where food was scarce. Camp Hollis's goal was not only to be a place where children could enjoy fun and games—something they normally would not be able to do because of their financial circumstances—but also a place where they could achieve healthy weight gain.

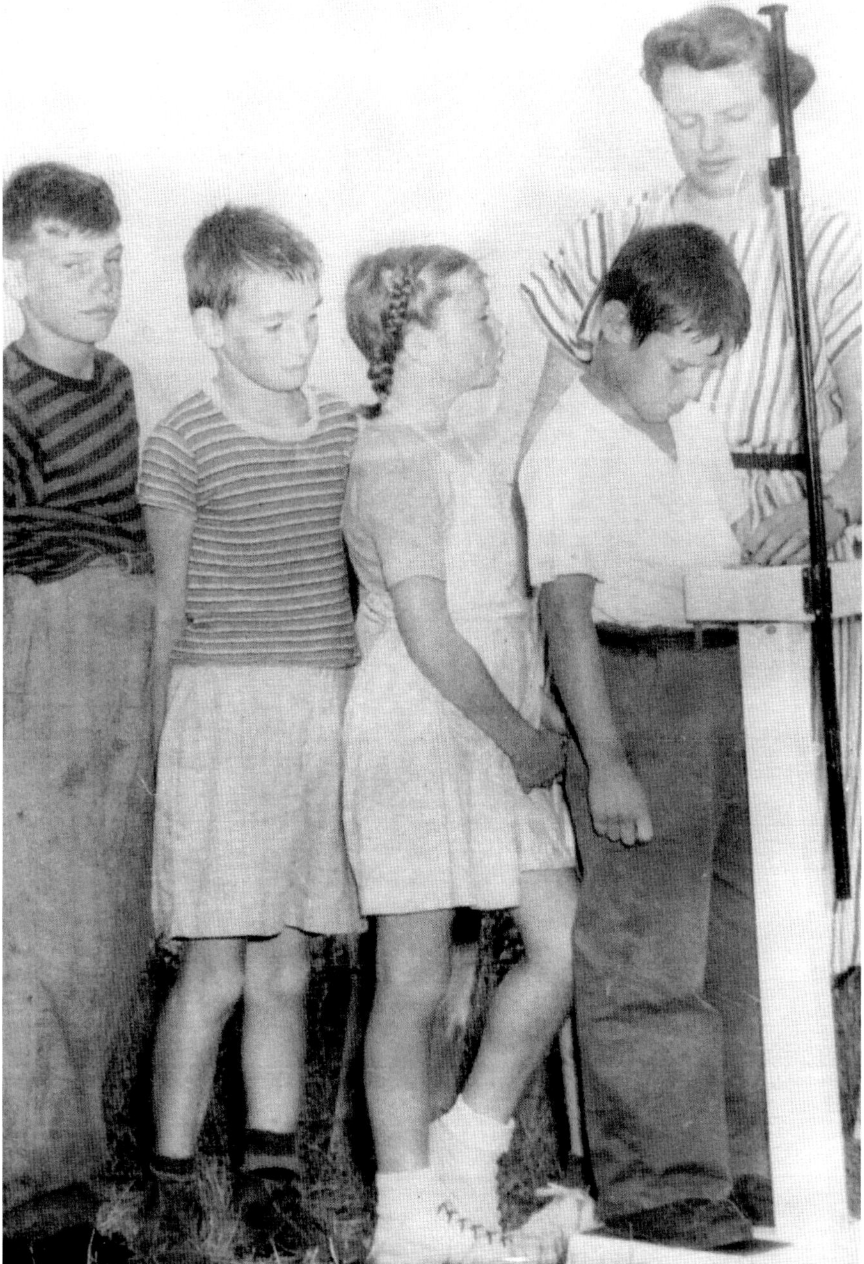

The campers' weight progress was charted on a weekly basis. A full-time nurse also provided lessons of basic hygiene such as teeth brushing and keeping clean.

The kitchen staff took a special pride in providing tasty, well-balanced meals. Campers marveled at the large portions. The smiles were as broad as the watermelon slices they were eating!

It was often nurses at local schools who would make recommendations of campers to Camp Hollis's committee. Camp Hollis was a fun time, but it also promoted good health habits by experiencing the outdoors with all its excitement and mystery.

Camp Hollis offered various types of recreation for its campers. New games and equipment were enjoyed by the campers as well as old standbys such as capture the flag, hide-and-seek and baseball.

The playground equipment on the grounds was something novel to most of the children. Clinton Hulett, a resident of the Oswego Children's Home in the 1940s and '50s, described the recreation at the home as minimal. Camp Hollis, conversely, was seen as an amusement haven.

The camp became a place where children could play team sports, as there were so many fellow campers and counselors willing to lead them. Counselors were flexible so that the rules of the game could always fit the situation.

Some games didn't need any equipment, just a counselor's imagination.

Many games, such as kick the can, could be learned at camp and then played at home.

Group swimming was a rare treat for the children. Games, water races and other activities made swim time one of the most anticipated parts of each day.

Swimming with a buddy was an integral part of the water safety program. While helping the lifeguards to keep track of all swimmers, the children also learned to watch out for one another.

Clinton Hulett: "There was a lot of advantage out there. You learned to get along with other kids. At camp, you made friends and there was no pressure to get along…you just did."

Keith Greeney, a camper in 1953 and 1954, recalls: "You learned to get along and work with other campers."

As the years progressed, many of the same children came back time and time again. Returning to camp year after year was a sort of homecoming.

Ted Baker, who attended Camp Hollis in 1952, remembers: "The opportunity to go to Camp Hollis made me feel very special."

Right: Camp Hollis became fertile ground for its campers to have the opportunity to create strong friendships. Those friendships were cultivated over several summers of fun, games and foundational life lessons.

Below: Camp Hollis offered children a unique perspective on life, one of opportunity and self-worth.

Within a single camp session, the children would enjoy a variety of first-time events. Playing archery, hiking on wooded trails and attending a large outdoor picnic were exciting memories.

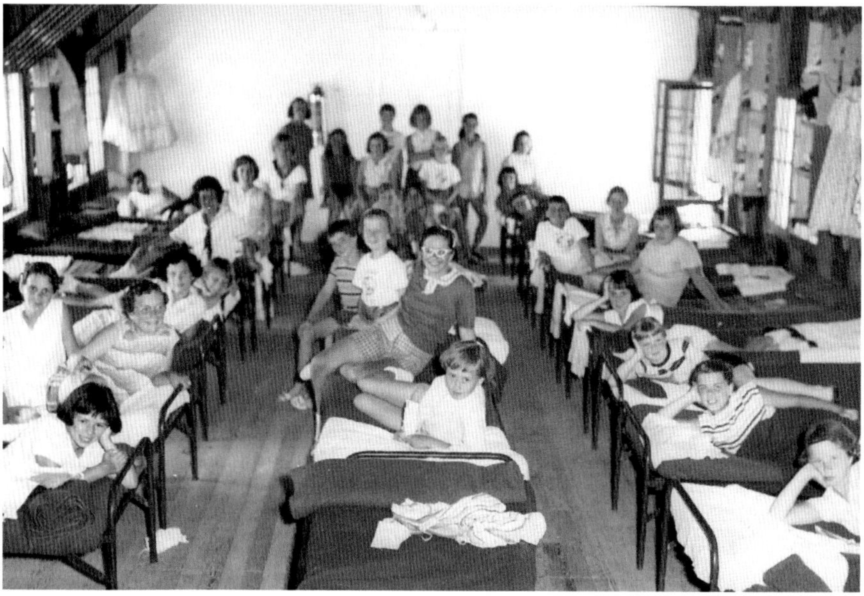

The dorms (and later cabin units) created "families." Led by counselor "Mom" and "Dad," the campers developed deep attachments to their "parents" and "siblings."

Keith Greeney, who attended Camp Hollis in 1953 and 1954, claims that his experiences at Camp Hollis motivated him to graduate from high school. "It was a big thing in my family. Throughout the various positive experiences in my life, the one that sticks out the most is Camp Hollis; I say that very sincerely. I think if I had to give up any experiences, I would not give up Camp Hollis."

Many campers have since returned to Camp Hollis in their adulthood to visit the grounds and relive the wonderful memories they had there during their childhood.

Memories of learning to swing a bat, swim underwater or act in a skit made the Camp Hollis experience so important to many.

Providing a summer of fun and encouraging a happy outlook on life, Camp Hollis became a special part of each camper's life.

OPPORTUNITIES

The Camp's Programs

Camp Hollis was not unlike other traditional summer camps. The core of its program offered the basics of summer fun: swimming, hiking, archery, basketball and arts and crafts. What set it apart from other camps was that it provided those typical camp experiences for children who would otherwise not have had such an opportunity. This made the activities special because for many of the children, they were experiencing them for their first time. Baseball games seemed like big-league tournaments. Arts and crafts projects were treasures to bring home to share with parents, siblings and close friends. Family-style meals were akin to fine dining at a fancy restaurant. Dances felt like senior proms.

The programs offered at Camp Hollis provided a rich experience. Here a first-time camper could experience, as one former camper recalled, "being treated like a king." Shooting an arrow during archery class, riding in a canoe and looking through binoculars far down the lakeshore opened up a new world for these children. Many children discovered a new sense of themselves at Camp Hollis. Those discoveries enriched their family experiences upon returning home and, for some, strongly influenced their educational and career choices.

The *Palladium-Times*, which covered the Camp Hollis program on a weekly basis with lots of photos, published the following program schedule:

7:00 am—Counselors rise
7:15 am—Counselors supervise the campers in getting dressed, washing
7:55 am—Flag raising, salute to the Flag, singing of America
8:00 am—Prayers, breakfast
8:30 am—Campers make their beds, clean room
9:00 am—Inspection of dormitories

9:00–10:00 am—Free time on playground
10:00–11:45 am—Swimming instruction
11:45 am–12:00 pm—Counselors supervise dressing
12:00–12:45 pm—Prayer, dinner
12:45–2:15 pm—Rest period
2:15–4:45 pm—Swimming
4:45–5:00 pm—Counselors supervise dressing for supper
5:00–5:45 pm—Prayers and supper
5:45–7:30 pm—Supervised games on the play area
7:30–8:00 pm—Ready for bed
8:00 pm—Everybody quiet
9:00 pm—Everybody asleep
The following activities were used on cloudy or rainy weather: Boxing, wrestling, movies, letter writing, story telling, novelty stunts and indoor games. An amateur show has been the feature entertainment for the last night at camp.

A report to the OCHA Camp committee stated: "The program was eating [the committee proudly reported that each child had one and a half quarts of milk a day], swimming 6 hours a day when the lake conditions permitted (morning, afternoon, evening), hiking, hot dog roast on the beach, dancing, singing, crafts, movies, swings, baseball."

Camp Hollis's backyard, Lake Ontario, is what made the camp special for a lot of its campers. The camp, on the lake, provided an abundance of water activities. When enthusiasm for the water wasn't satisfied with three trips to the lake a day, counselors developed a fourth: campers had an opportunity to participate in an early morning swim club!

Campfires were a natural part of camp and the location of the camp near wooded area gave counselors an opportunity to create thrilling nighttime stories. Some stories involved visits from local ghosts and counselors took turns donning mops, seaweed and leaves and hiding among the trees. At appropriate times, moans and shrieks were added. Campers would scream in delight. A favorite ghost, George Hollis, developed over the years to tell a story with a moral that encouraged good behavior from the campers. Campfires also blended dozens of voices together as campers and staff shared traditional and novelty songs. Counselors brought unique talents to this activity—Jean Galvin put the words to a special camp song in 1954: "Hollis will shine tonight, Hollis will shine. All down the line tonight, Hollis will shine. We're all dressed up tonight. Don't we look fine. When the sun goes down and the moon comes up, Hollis will shine!"

The lucky campers were treated to a variety of special events during their stay. With cooperation from local businesses and civic clubs, the children took field trips to Fair Haven, the Oswego Speedway and Scriba Firemen's Field Days. Treats like a fish fry from Cahill's, walks to the ice cream stand and fun movie nights featuring Hopalong Cassidy thrilled the campers. Director Bob Bellinger remembers, "One time a counselor was getting married. I made arrangements with 'Dynamite' Gould's bus service to transport everyone at Camp to the church to watch the ceremony. We took up a whole section of St. Mary's Church and were quite a sight!"

While Camp Hollis provided myriad activities, important life lessons were remembered long after the summers at Camp Hollis had ended. Children learned the order of a healthy life in daily chores like morning cleanup. The campers spent time each morning making their beds. During the afternoon on the day they arrived, the counselor in charge showed campers how to make their beds using "hospital corners." When the director inspected the dorms, he would try to make a quarter bounce off the cots—that was the measuring tool he used to see if the blankets were tucked in appropriately. Parents were amazed when their children returned home having learned to make their bed and clean a toilet. Table manners were practiced while piping-hot dishes of meat and mashed potatoes were passed from hungry person to hungry person. Waiting in line for a turn at bat or to ride the playground's equipment instilled valuable lessons for these children.

It was through games, activities and social events that those important lessons were learned. Campers returned home with stories of "what happened each day" at Camp. Within the span of two or three weeks, campers developed an understanding of how a productive and enjoyable day happens. Participating in activities that were presented and enjoyed with positive role models taught children the benefit of healthy fun. Upon returning home, these fundamentals were then carried out in other arenas—in friendships, classrooms and family situations.

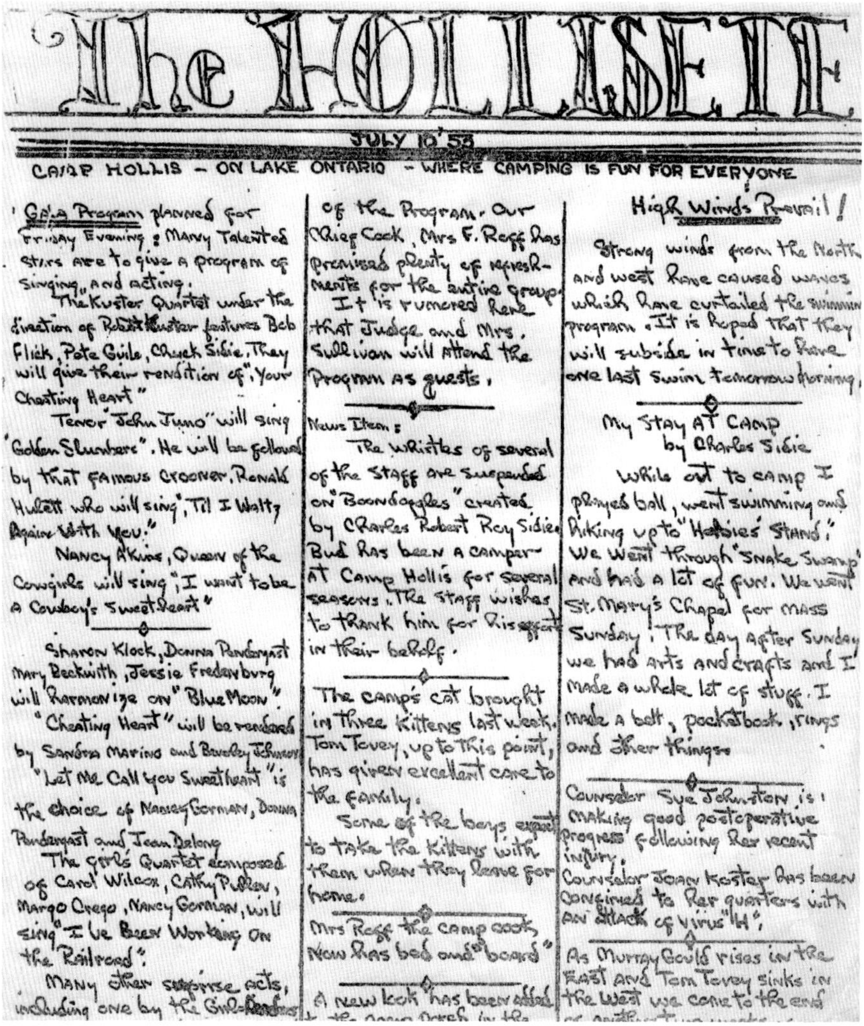

The HOLLISETTE

JULY 10 '53

CAMP HOLLIS – ON LAKE ONTARIO – WHERE CAMPING IS FUN FOR EVERYONE

Gala Program planned for Friday Evening: Many Talented stars are to give a program of singing, and acting.

The Kuster Quartet under the direction of Robert Kuster features Bob Flick, Pete Guile, Chuck Sidie. They will give their rendition of "Your Cheating Heart"

Tenor "John Juno" will sing "Golden Slumbers". He will be followed by that famous crooner, Ronald Hulett who will sing "Til I Waltz Again With You."

Nancy Akins, Queen of the Cowgirls will sing "I want to be a Cowboy's Sweetheart"

Sharon Klock, Donna Pendergast, Mary Beckwith, Jessie Fredenburg will harmonize on "Blue Moon".

"Cheating Heart" will be rendered by Sandra Marino and Beverley Johnson.

"Let Me Call you Sweetheart" is the choice of Nancy Gorman, Donna Pendergast and Jean Delong.

The girl's Quartet composed of Carol Wilcox, Cathy Pullen, Margo Crego, Nancy Gorman, will sing "I've Been Working On the Railroad".

Many other surprise acts, including one by the Girl-[illegible] of the Program. Our Chief Cook, Mrs F. Ragg has promised plenty of refreshments for the entire group.

It is rumored here that Judge and Mrs. Sullivan will attend the Program as guests.

News Item:

The writtles of several of the staff are suspended on "Boondoggles" created by Charles Robert Roy Sidie. Bud has been a camper at Camp Hollis for several seasons. The staff wishes to thank him for his effort in their behalf.

The camp's cat brought in three kittens last week. Tom Tovey, up to this point, has given excellent care to the family.

Some of the boys expect to take the kittens with them when they leave for home.

Mrs Ragg the camp cook now has bed and "board"

A new look has been added ...

High Winds Prevail!

Strong winds from the North and west have caused waves which have curtailed the swimming program. It is hoped that they will subside in time to have one last swim tomorrow morning.

My Stay At Camp
by Charles Sidie

While out to camp I played ball, went swimming and hiking up to "Hobies' Stand". We went through "Snake Swamp" and had a lot of fun. We went St. Mary's Chapel for mass Sunday. The day after Sunday we had arts and crafts and I made a whole lot of stuff. I made a belt, pocketbook, rings and other things.

Counselor Sue Johnston is making good postoperative progress following her recent injury.

Counselor Joan Koster has been confined to her quarters with an attack of virus "H".

As Murray Gould rises in the East and Tom Tovey sinks in the West we come to the end ...

While most children who were eligible to attend Camp Hollis had experienced some sort of hardship, time there is remembered by the campers to be one of great fun. Camp Hollis's newspaper, the *Hollisette*, outlines the various activities the camp had to offer.

Developing a recreational program in a largely wooded area was a challenge. Playground equipment was gradually installed among the trees and shrubbery.

Working with a limited budget, the camp began with the most popular playground equipment first. Swing sets were utilized nearly every available moment.

Baseball was quite popular. The ball field was one of the first large play areas installed. It accommodated hours of baseball, softball and kickball.

Considering Camp Hollis's prime location, right on the shores of Lake Ontario, many of the camp's most popular activities revolved around the water.

The campgrounds, located so close to the shoreline, made good use of the expansive waterfront. Counselors were trained to be lifeguards and were stationed along the beach in order to keep a close watch on the campers.

For the more adventurous camper, an extremely popular lake activity was created in the early years of Camp Hollis. The Polar Bear Club, in which campers could start swimming before the scheduled wakeup time, is remembered with fondness by many. Campers who participated every day in the Polar Bear Club received a certificate at the end of the camp session.

A playground slide was placed on the banks of the lake in order to create a makeshift waterslide. Campers would wait in long lines in order to participate in this popular waterfront activity.

Lake Ontario came to represent much more for Camp Hollis campers. As Clinton Hulett recalled: "A lot of kids learned to swim out there. After I learned, I was able to give swimming lessons when I became a counselor. There was a lot of advantage out there."

Right: Campers and counselors alike set a goal to learn to swim while attending Camp Hollis. Success with these goals transcended into strong personal development skills as children matured to adulthood.

Below: In addition to swimming, campers could also go rafting, boating and tubing. Here a counselor is advising a group ready to go out on the water on a typical Camp Hollis summer day.

When a heat wave moved through the area, the lifeguards arranged for extra swim times. One treat for the campers were night swims. Campers stayed cool as they watched the sun set over the lake.

The myriad opportunities offered by the lake made it difficult for children to part with it after their respective activity was over. One camper recalls "freezing our tails off! Our lips were turning blue and shivering, but I didn't want to come out of the water!"

The traditional Camp Hollis Hop was one of the most popular events during the camp sessions. Each "Hop" featured a theme song, which was most often a popular song of that era.

Counselors hang streamers from the ceiling for the Hollis Hop. The dance was something to look forward to for the older campers, who were in their early adolescent years.

Judge Sullivan dances happily with the campers during the Hollis Hop. Counselors and other staff often encouraged shy children to participate in the dances and enjoy the party atmosphere.

A counselor places decorations for the Royal Court on the wall of the main building in preparation for the Hollis Hop. Announcement of the court was often awaited with great anticipation.

A camper demonstrates a hula dance at the Hollis Hop's "Tropical Theme" dance, the theme chosen for this particular week.

Camp director Bob Bellinger dances with a camper at the Hollis Hop in front of an audience of enthusiastic onlookers in order to break the ice at the dance.

For many children, the Hollis Hop was their first social event. Getting up the nerve to ask someone to dance was a daunting task for many campers and counselors often helped out.

While "dressing up" for the Hollis Hop was not a requirement, the excitement of the dance encouraged everyone to look their best. Boys added extra applications of aftershave and the girls tried the latest hairdos on each other.

Pictured here is the Camp Hollis Royal Court. Each session ended with the crowning of the Camp Hollis King, Queen, Prince and Princess as voted by the staff, who decided which campers would receive the honor.

Special acknowledgements like being crowned as "royalty" were often life changing for a camper. Years later, former campers remember such moments as tremendous self-esteem builders.

A counselor announces the names of the lucky campers chosen to be on the Royal Court. The decision of who would be named was a difficult one and was seen as the highlight of the dance.

Skit Night, where Camp Hollis campers showcased their more creative talents, was an event to look forward to. Campers of all ages would take the stage and perform various forms of entertainment for the enjoyment of the rest of camp.

Skit Night was a rare opportunity for the children to cultivate certain talents. Many of the acts performed were solo acts that the campers had fun preparing.

Other campers teamed up to provide comedy skits for the other campers and staff. Many of these skits mimicked the popular movie stars of the day.

Campers performed skits in their special groups, often called "tribes." The bond with the select eight or nine campers over the two-week sessions created a sense of community, a special type of family.

Activities often echoed the popular television shows and motion pictures of the day. Staff and campers would take turns entertaining each other with these adaptations.

Above: Even though all of Camp Hollis's attendees were from the Oswego County region, many of the campers did not know each other and created firm bonds at camp. Here, two female campers perform a lighthearted skit together.

Right: Outdoor events provided most of the camp activity on the schedule. Some were traditional sports that the campers had participated in at home or school.

Counselors lead a spirited game of baseball for the campers.

After the end of World War II, organized team sports began to gain popularity throughout the country. Because many of them followed big-league games, staff members created their own versions of those games at camp.

This popular playground activity brought much joy for the campers. Campers used imagination to create high-flying hours of fun.

The opportunity to participate in activities from morning until evening was a treat for many children. One exciting activity followed another. By the end of the day, most campers had little trouble falling asleep.

The campgrounds were a perfect environment for nightly campfires. Campers would collect driftwood from the beach as counselors constructed mammoth bonfires. Songs and skits followed.

Boxing was both widely accepted and popular at Camp Hollis! Pictured here are two counselors horsing around, David O'Brien and Adeline Mirandes.

Right: While boxing was only open to the male campers, the general atmosphere of Camp Hollis was rather lighthearted and easygoing. Here, two campers, a girl and a boy, "play" box.

Below: Counselors were built-in coaches and referees. Their guidance during games and activities made the games fair for everyone.

Roy Abbott, who attended Camp Hollis in 1952 and 1953, recalls the activities at Camp Hollis as "things I always really liked. All of the things they had going on there with the swimming, the woods, it was all great. I liked the outdoors and camp was the outdoors."

The acres of wooded area that surrounded the campgrounds offered plenty of opportunities for creating a trail system. Hikes were a daily part of the camp's program, and it was along these trails that the legend of George Hollis's "quicksand" and the "old bus" were told.

The mealtime was the core of each camper's daily schedule at Camp Hollis.

Breakfasts at Camp Hollis were a special treat. One camper remembers, "You'd get cereal and toast and pancakes and those sorts of things. There was a lot, as much as you wanted."

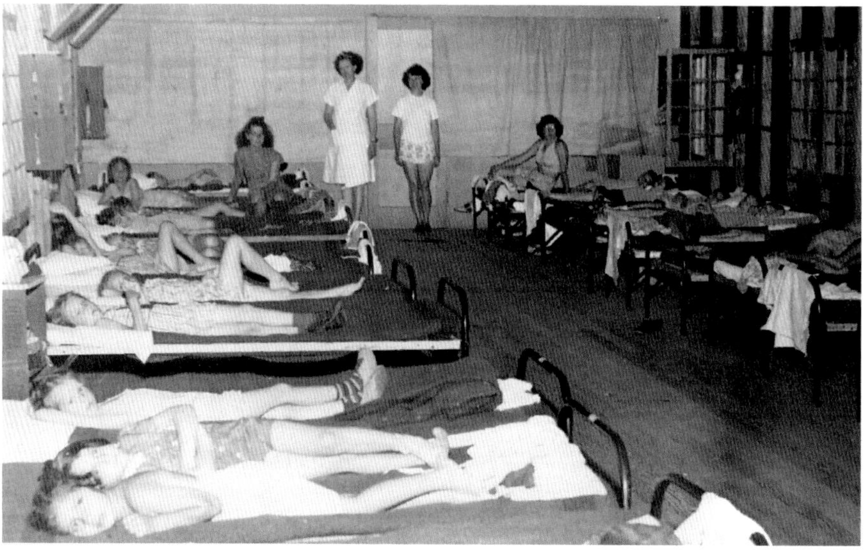

Not as popular as meal time, yet still very important to the Camp Hollis regimen, was the rest period. Throughout the day, there were scattered opportunities for free time for the campers. Many opted for a quick afternoon nap during this time.

Arts and crafts, of course, was a popular activity. Not only were children able to draw, paint and color, but they were also able to make items that they could take home. Some of these items included potholders, various stitch work, candle holders and more.

Many of the children looked forward to enjoying religious services on Sunday. The Catholic campers were taken to St. Ann's, with the Knights of Columbus providing the transportation.

There was a Sunday service provided by a clergyman from the Ministerial Association for the Protestant campers on the campgrounds.

The various recreational outlets that Camp Hollis provided allowed for its campers to enjoy many activities.

The great care, fun and games brought children back to Camp Hollis year after year. Children waited in anticipation each spring for the letter in the mail inviting them back to Camp Hollis.

Year after year, generation upon generation, the magic of Camp Hollis became an establishment in Oswego County. With a mention of its name, memories flood back to rekindle in the young camper's heart the chance for all children to enjoy life.

EPILOGUE

It can be argued that not much has changed at Camp Hollis since 1946. Today campers and staff live in cabins instead of dorms, and have a pool for swimming rather than the lake. But the sun still sets over that lake, catching the camp's collective breath each night. The daily schedule looks almost identical to that of the first year, from morning cleanup and evening flag lowering. There is something both comforting and mysterious in seeing such similarities in place at Camp Hollis after sixty-two years.

We are lucky to have camp programs in this ultra-modern world we live in. The need for opportunities to spend recreational time outdoors has become a national crisis, as children spend increasing amounts of time with electronic equipment. A brand-new phenomenon, known as "nature deficit disorder," is causing alarm in those who are in child-care professions. Children deprived of healthy exposure to the out-of-doors show a decline in cognitive and socialization skills.

Another similarity to 1946 in today's socially charged era is that children still look to their elders as they strive to understand the world. Young adults, especially, hold particular attraction to the children. There is something magical about a counselor—they are not a parent, and not an older sibling, but a caring adult nonetheless—and oftentimes they are someone the camper wants to be "just like." The fuel that fires Sullivan's dream after all these years are the young adults who continue to make up the majority of each summer's staff. No camp program can be successful without the individuals who create and execute them.

At the beginning of each summer, a team of young adults arrives to Camp ready to change the world. The energy that these talented counselors and staff members collectively offer the program ignites the activities. When young adults discover the Hollis mission and adopt it as their own, miracles truly can happen. It is a miracle indeed to behold how quickly a troubled spirit can be lifted when someone who demonstrates concern and care enters the child's life. A week at Camp can introduce a new vision of the world that can grow and last a lifetime.

This is the mission that all camps strive to achieve. Hollis is no different, and it is working hard to survive the shifting cultural climate. What sets Camp Hollis apart from other camps and makes it a rare gem in Oswego County is the legacy that Judge Eugene Sullivan created when he founded a program for children who would not have been able to experience organized summer recreation without it. Oswego County's commitment to Sullivan's dream, through both lean and bountiful economic times, is remarkable in today's world. More often than not, municipalities and government support systems are downsizing and reducing services as costs skyrocket. However, year after year, the county and the community support the camp, continuing the dream. Although fees have been charged since 2002 for children to attend Camp, the fee structure is both reasonable and considerate of each family's unique circumstances. The strong philanthropic belief of the Friends of Camp Hollis, a nonprofit organization providing financial resources to the camp, allows those in need to still send children to Camp at no cost to the family. Additionally, several local agencies sponsor children to attend the sessions. Churches and educational institutions work with the camp staff to make sure the children who greatly need the positive social environment find a way to attend. Private individuals, from the very young to those still young at heart, offer generous donations to help one child at a time have a summer vacation to remember.

The dream that Judge Sullivan had over sixty years ago has as much reason to be believed in today as it did then. No matter how sophisticated our culture becomes, the same activities that thrilled children in 1946 continue to do so in 2008. The skits at the campfire bring ripples of laughter that mix with the waves on the lake. Themed dances continue to muster the best gossip throughout the Camp community, with campers wondering who will dance with whom. Campers still peek through the dining hall window to smell the wonderful aromas coming from the kitchen and see what will be served for breakfast. The concepts of teamwork and the fair treatment of others continue to be practiced daily throughout the summer. Judge Sullivan's vision was the catalyst that brought great change to Oswego County in 1946. How far that vision has reached in 2008 is a testimonial to the countless staff whose goal it was to make Camp Hollis a better world for children. Every counselor and camper, yesterday and today, who has come to love Camp Hollis has this man's vision to thank.

ABOUT THE AUTHORS

Jim Farfaglia attended Camp Hollis as a child and worked there as a counselor and site director while in college, where he earned a teaching degree. He is currently employed by Oswego County as Camp Hollis's year-round director.

Alysa Koloms was born in Chicago, Illinois, where she spent most of her childhood, and is a recent graduate of the State University of Oswego with a degree in history. Her research interests include Modern American History, specifically that of the immediate post–World War II era. Alysa is currently attending Hofstra University.

Jane Ann (Sullivan) Spellman is the daughter of Camp Hollis founder Eugene F. Sullivan. She graduated from Smith College in Northampton, Massachusetts, and worked for both the Girl Scouts and the United Fund of Syracuse, New York. She retired after twenty two years as the director of Herkimer County Historical Society.